GETTING TO KNOW
THE U.S. PRESIDENTS

Z A C H A R Y
TAYLOR

TWELFTH PRESIDENT
1849 – 1850

WRITTEN AND ILLUSTRATED BY MIKE VENEZIA

CHILDREN'S PRESS®
A DIVISION OF SCHOLASTIC INC.
NEW YORK   TORONTO   LONDON   AUCKLAND   SYDNEY
MEXICO CITY   NEW DELHI   HONG KONG
DANBURY, CONNECTICUT

Reading Consultant: Nanci R. Vargus, Ed.D., Assistant Professor, School of Education, University of Indianapolis

Historical Consultant: Marc J. Selverstone, Ph.D., Assistant Professor, Miller Center of Public Affairs, University of Virginia

Colorist for illustrations: Dave Ludwig

Library of Congress Cataloging-in-Publication Data

Venezia, Mike.
  Zachary Taylor : twelfth president, 1849-1850 / written and illustrated by Mike Venezia — 1st ed.
    p. cm. — (Getting to know the U.S. presidents)
  ISBN 0-516-22617-7 (lib. bdg.)   0-516-27486-4 (pbk.)
  1. Taylor, Zachary, 1784-1850—Juvenile literature. 2. Presidents—United States—Biography—Juvenile literature. I. Title. II. Series.

  E422.V46 2004
  973.6'3'092—dc22

                                    2004007206

A portrait of Zachary Taylor by James Lambdin (National Portrait Gallery, Smithsonian Institution, Washington, D.C.)

Zachary Taylor was the twelfth president of the United States. He was born on November 24, 1784, near Barboursville, Virginia. Zachary didn't have any experience to be president. He was elected president mainly because he was a famous war hero and the most popular man in the country.

Zachary Taylor spent almost forty years of
his life in the United States Army. He fought
in wars against American Indians, the British,
and the Mexican Army. Zachary Taylor was
known to fight right alongside his men.
Often, he and his men were outnumbered
by enemies.

Because he was so clever and brave, Zachary never lost even one battle while he was in command. His men respected him so much that they gave Zachary a neat nickname. They started calling him Old Rough and Ready.

Zachary Taylor was born during his family's journey from Virginia to Kentucky. Zachary's father owned some land in Beargrass Creek, a frontier area near Louisville, Kentucky. He thought it would be the perfect place to start a farm and raise his family.

Zachary Taylor's boyhood home in Kentucky

The Taylors built and lived in a small log cabin. Over the years they added on to the cabin until it became a large, fancy house. Zachary and his brothers and sisters worked hard on the farm. They cut down trees and plowed fields right alongside the slaves Mr. Taylor owned. The Taylors became very successful.

Children on frontier farms had so much work to do that they had very little time for schooling. Even as a grown-up, Zachary always had trouble with his spelling and grammar. His penmanship was very poor, too. Zachary learned a lot about other things, though. He was an excellent horseback rider, fisherman, and hunter. Zachary had perfect aim with his musket.

At one point, neighbors in the area got together and hired a teacher for their children. Elisha Ayer was a good instructor.

Once, a famous backswoodsman named Lewis Wetzel visited the area. Lew Wetzel

Lewis Wetzel

taught the local boys how to survive in
the wilderness. Zachary learned important
things that would help him later in his life.

In the late 1700s, the Kentucky frontier was a pretty dangerous place. Sometimes American Indians, angry about white settlers taking their land, would attack settlers' homes. Not only did Zachary have to worry about his house being attacked, but he and his brothers and sisters had to try to fall asleep to the sound of howling wolves!

One of Zachary's favorite things to do while he was growing up was to play army with his friends. He also loved listening to stories his father told about his adventures as a soldier during the Revolutionary War.

It didn't surprise anyone when Zachary told his parents he wanted to join the army. Zachary felt that the skills he learned growing up in the wilderness would be all he needed to be a good soldier. Mr. and Mrs. Taylor agreed. In 1808, at the age of twenty-three, Zachary Taylor joined the United States Army. He was given the rank of first lieutenant.

A portrait of
Margaret Smith Taylor

Zachary Taylor began his military career by
recruiting new members for the army. He also
helped build new forts in different frontier areas.

Once, Zachary got a serious disease called
yellow fever. He had to return home to
Beargrass Creek to recover. When he felt better,
Zachary traveled to nearby Louisville to attend
dances, parties, and dinners. During one of his
fun trips, he met Margaret Smith.

Margaret, whose nickname was Peggy, was a wealthy, well-educated girl visiting from Maryland. Zachary and Peggy fell in love right away. After dating for a while, they decided to get married in 1810. As a gift, Zachary's father gave the couple 324 acres (131 hectares) of land.

Fort Harrison in the Indiana Territory was one of the wilderness outposts Zachary Taylor commanded in the early 1800s.

Zachary and Peggy built a new home and started farming their land right away. It wasn't long, though, before Zachary was called back to his army job.

Zachary moved from one frontier outpost to another. He did a first-rate job building forts, recruiting men, and training men to be good soldiers.

Zachary became known as a skillful leader and was soon promoted to fort commander. He often brought his family along to live with him at the different forts under his command.

A woodcut showing American Indians along the Ohio River in the early 1800s

There was plenty of work for U.S. soldiers in the early 1800s. American Indians were growing more and more angry. They had a pretty good reason for being upset, too. For years, the United States government had made peace with some American Indian peoples by promising the Indians that they could keep their land.

When thousands of pioneers began moving west and settling on Indian lands, the U.S. government didn't always keep the promises, or treaties, they had made. Many Indian leaders decided to fight the settlers to keep them from taking over their land. The U.S. Army was called in to keep the peace. Zachary Taylor worked hard at this. Though he often fought Indians, he also worked to protect Indian lands from invading white settlers.

Pioneers settling in the Northwest Territory along the Ohio River in the early 1800s

In 1812, things got even busier for Zachary Taylor and the U.S. Army when the United States and Great Britain went to war for a second time. The British had been stopping American ships and kidnapping sailors. They then forced these sailors to be in the British navy. Also, after the Revolutionary War, the British were supposed to leave territories in North America. Many of them stayed, however. They built forts and hoped to get some of the land back for England.

American Indians battling U.S. troops during the War of 1812

A war seemed to be the only way to stop the British. During the War of 1812, the British army started supplying American Indians with weapons. They encouraged the Indians to attack U.S. settlers and soldiers. Zachary Taylor was right there, fighting to protect settlers during the war.

The War of 1812 ended in 1814. There was no real winner. Both sides agreed to stop fighting. Zachary then decided to take a year off from the army to work on his farm. When he returned to the army, he traveled to different states and territories to set up and command forts. In 1832, he was promoted to the high rank of colonel.

In Illinois and Wisconsin, Zachary defeated the Fox and Sac Indians and their fierce leader Chief Black Hawk. Zachary Taylor was starting to become well known throughout the country for his heroic actions.

Even though Taylor was very popular, there were some people who criticized him. For much of his career, Zachary refused to wear a regular military uniform. Instead, he wore a floppy straw hat, long cotton coat, and comfortable, baggy pants. It was also known that he liked to drink whiskey. Worst of all, he liked to chew tobacco. Some Congressmen and military leaders thought Colonel Taylor was a sloppy and rude military man.

Colonel Zachary Taylor didn't really care what people thought of him. He cared only about what he did best, which was to win wars. In 1837, Colonel Taylor won an important battle against the Seminole Indians in Florida. The next year, he was promoted to the rank of brigadier general. For the next few years, General Taylor took command of military forces in Florida, Oklahoma, Arkansas, and Louisiana.

An engraving showing Colonel Taylor (on horse) fighting the Seminole during the 1837 Battle of Okeechobee

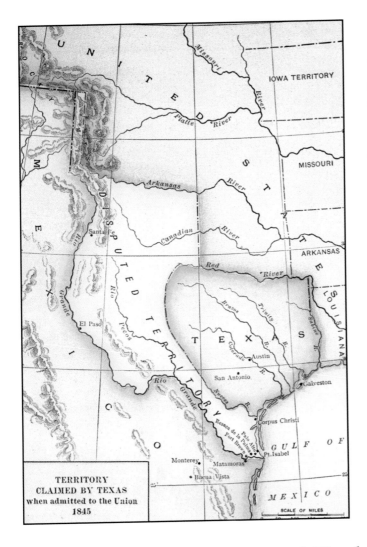

The orange section of this map shows Texas's borders when Texas became a state in 1845. The yellow section is the portion of land that the United States and Mexico continued to fight over.

Then, in 1846, General Taylor got orders to bring his troops to Texas. For years, the United States and Mexico had quarreled over the Texas Territory. When Texas was finally made a state in 1845, the two countries then began arguing over where the southern border should be. The United States and Mexico became so angry with each other that they went to war.

A painting by William Henry Powell showing General Zachary Taylor at the Battle of Buena Vista

It was during the Mexican War that General Zachary Taylor really showed what an excellent leader he was. General Taylor won battle after battle against the Mexican army. During the Battle of Buena Vista, the famous Mexican General Antonio Santa Anna led twenty thousand soldiers against General Taylor's six thousand men. General Taylor sat on his favorite horse, Old Whitey, giving commands and encouraging his men.

During the fight, one bullet tore through Taylor's sleeve. Another bullet shot off a coat button! In the end, General Taylor and his troops won the battle. Zachary became a national hero and the most popular man in the country. Songs were written about him and "Zachary Taylor for President" clubs started popping up all over the United States.

A campaign poster showing Zachary Taylor on his horse, Old Whitey

At first, Zachary Taylor was surprised. He never wanted anything to do with being president. But his friends kept trying to convince him that he would make a great president. Since he was used to being in charge and enjoyed difficult challenges, Zachary eventually agreed to run for the job. In 1848, Zachary Taylor was elected president of the United States.

Zachary quit his army job and moved to
Washington, D.C., with his wife and children.
Old Whitey came along, too. President Taylor's
favorite horse was given special privileges.
Old Whitey was even allowed to graze on the
White House lawn.

When President Taylor began his new job, there were a lot of problems to deal with. The most serious problem was what to do about slavery in the United States.

During this time, the nation included fifteen southern states. The people of these states wanted to continue to use slaves to help run their tobacco and cotton plantations.

An engraving showing slaves returning from the fields of a sugar plantation at the end of the day

The nation also had fifteen northern states, whose people thought slavery was wrong and should be stopped. The members of the U.S. Congress had to decide if slavery should be allowed in new territories the United States had won from Mexico.

Since President Taylor owned slaves himself, southerners expected him to be on their side. Zachary Taylor surprised people, however. He thought that the people of the new territories should decide for themselves whether to have slavery. President Taylor's point of view angered many southerners.

Some southern leaders were so upset with
President Taylor they thought their states
might be better off seceding from, or leaving,
the United States. When President Taylor
found out about their plans, he was furious!
The president said if any state dared to leave

the Union, he would have the army hunt
down their leaders and have them put
to death. Above all else, President Taylor
believed that keeping the states together
as one country was absolutely necessary.

A photograph of Zachary Taylor in military uniform

After President Taylor made his feelings clear, the members of Congress began working on a solution before anyone got hurt. The Compromise of 1850 kept the United States together until the Civil War started eleven years later.

Unfortunately, Zachary Taylor was president for only sixteen months. In 1850, after attending Fourth of July celebrations, he became terribly sick with stomach problems. He died five days later. Over 100,000 shocked and saddened people lined the streets at President Taylor's funeral. They came to honor their favorite hero for the last time.